DR. J

DR. J

BY BILL GUTMAN

tempo
books

GROSSET & DUNLAP, Inc.
Publishers   New York
A FILMWAYS COMPANY

PICTURE CREDIT
Cover: Joe DiMaggio

Dorothy Affa/Sport Magazine: p. 86; Lawrence Berman: pp. 55,
62, 65, 67, 68, 72, 82, 84, 85, 87; J. DiMaggio/J. Kalish:
p. 61; Ebony Magazine: p. 89; Kevin Fitzgerald/Sport
Magazine: p. 4; Focus on Sports/Duomo: p. 40; Carl Ska-
lak/Sport Magazine: p. vi; University of Massachusetts:
pp. 25, 27; UPI: pp. 17, 52, 76, 80; Ron West: pp. 32,
35, 36.

Photo Research By Gary Wohl

CONTENTS

CHAPTER ONE

THAT LITTLE SOMETHING EXTRA

Nicknames play a big part in all sports. Almost every player, sooner or later, is given a nickname. In many cases, the nickname is used more than the real name. People know many of these nicknames, some better than others. But perhaps the best-known nickname in all of sports is also one of the simplest.

The Doctor!

By now it's no secret. The man they call the Doctor is Julius Erving. And he is perhaps the most exciting basketball player in the whole long history of the sport.

Julius Erving seems to have that little extra something. Maybe it's the ability to jump a little higher or get that clutch basket or make that super move or invent a new way to slam-dunk. Or maybe it's all of those things put together. For the Doctor is without a doubt the player most hoop fans all across the country want to see. And he rarely disappoints them. It seems that every time he steps out on the court, Julius invents another way to play the game.

From 1971 to 1976, the Doctor played in the American Basketball Association (ABA). That was the new league that was trying to compete with the older National Basketball Association (NBA). First Julius played with the Virginia Squires, then with the New York Nets. It was always said that a new league needs a strong team in New York if it is going to work.

Well, all Julius did was lead the Nets to two ABA championships in three years. And during those three years he was the league's Most Valuable Player each time and its playoff MVP twice.

There were other outstanding players in the ABA, too. But one by one they seemed to be jumping over to the NBA. It seemed as though the ABA would not survive. Most people admitted that the one man holding the entire league together was Doctor J.

In fact, during the final year of the ABA's life, its commissioner, former NBA great Dave DeBusschere, said it all. "There are athletes who

are known as the franchise," said DeBusschere, "but Julius isn't the franchise, he's the league."

When the two leagues finally merged before the 1976-77 season, everyone was excited. Only four ABA teams survived to join the NBA. But all the outstanding ABA players were coming. That meant that more people than ever would be able to see Doctor J and his magic show. And because Julius played in New York, that would be even better. There would be a great rivalry between Julius and the Nets, and the older NBA New York Knickerbockers.

But things never seem to work out quite the way people like to see them. Before the season started, Doctor J got into the first controversy of his career. He wanted the

Julius Erving—the Doctor, Dr. J—is named Performer of the Year in 1976 by Sport *Magazine.*

Nets to give him a new contract. They said he still had four years to go on his old one. So the Doctor didn't come to camp. As the preseason games started, the league's most advertised player was a holdout.

It was a strange position for Julius to be in. Besides being a great athlete, he was also known as a great person. Everyone who met him liked him. He was friendly to reporters and spent a good deal of time helping youngsters. Even Roy Boe, the president of the Nets and the man Julius was holding out against, said, "Let there be no mistake about it. Julius Erving is one of the finest athletes and finest persons in America's sports history . . ."

The problem seemed to be the modern sports scene. Players were earning more money than ever before. Because there were two basketball leagues for a number of years, the hoop players made more money than anyone. Especially the super-stars. And most players had agents. They were men who tried to get new and better contracts from the team owners. In many cases this led to hard feelings.

Julius didn't play throughout the preseason. The Nets said they would not give him a new contract. Then, the day the regular season opened, the news hit the headlines. Julius Erving had been sold to the Philadelphia 76ers.

It was to be Julius' third pro team. The 76ers had some other star players. Most people figured that Julius would not be able to play the same kind of game he had with the Nets. But really to bring the Doctor's story up to date, it's necessary to go back a few years. That was when a thin youngster was discovering the game of basketball.

CHAPTER TWO

"THE DOCTOR" ARRIVES

No one called Julius by his nickname when he was born on February 22, 1950. He was just Julius Erving, a bouncing baby boy who lived in East Meadow, Long Island.

When Julius was just three, his father left the family, never to return. Julius grew up in a housing project in Hempstead, Long Island. He lived with his mother, Callie, his older sister, Alexis, and a young brother, Marvin.

It wasn't an easy life. Mrs. Erving had to go to work to feed and clothe her family. She worked as a domestic, which meant she spent her days cleaning other people's houses. The children were often left alone. That can be a bad situation. It's easy for youngsters to get in trouble when they spend a lot of alone on the streets.

But the Ervings were all good kids. They loved their mother and respected her. They knew how hard she worked for them and wouldn't do anything to disappoint her. They never gave her any real trouble.

When Julius was very young, he was small and thin. There was no sign that he'd become a great athlete. Then when he was 10 years old, he found the game of basketball.

It was at a Salvation Army Youth Center in Hempstead. The coach there was a man named Don Ryan. But he was more than just a coach. Don Ryan was interested in each and every boy who came to the Youth Center. Julius will never forget him.

"Don Ryan really opened my eyes," he says. "A lot of the guys at the Center came from broken homes, and Don taught us many things we would have ordinarily learned from our fathers. For instance, he showed us how to conduct ourselves in a strange environment."

And, of course, he also taught them basketball. Julius averaged 11 points a game at age 10. He seemed to take to the court game quickly. He wasn't that big or strong. But he moved very well and made many of the right moves by instinct.

Two years later he was the star of the Salvation Army team. He led them to the regional championship. But winning wasn't the only important thing that happened that year. The team had a chance to travel more. They often went to different communities in New York and Pennsylvania. It gave Julius the chance to see how other people lived.

"It was like looking to the other side of the fence," he remembers, "and seeing big houses, two cars, color TV sets, things like that. I began to wonder what you had to do to get them."

It didn't take Julius long to figure how he could get them. "I came to see that basketball represented an avenue for me to get out and see things. The more I saw, the more I wanted to see."

So Julius began to play really

hard. He was working on his game in earnest. Then when he was 13, Julius' life took a new turn. His mother married again, to a man named Stanley Lindsey. Soon after, the family moved to nearby Roosevelt, Long Island.

"We finally had our own home, a real home," remembers Julius. "But we had done well up to that point. I'd say my family survived because we had determination and a positive outlook. A lot of people I grew up with had the same chances I had, but they didn't have the same attitude. They just thought they'd do nothing, like everyone else—just hang around and that would be it. They didn't realize that it's your goals that determine what you're going to be. My goal had become basketball, and I worked hard to make things work out. I wasn't thinking about pro ball then.

But I knew basketball was a way for me to get a good education."

It was at Roosevelt High that Julius got his nickname. Most of the boys had some kind of nickname. For instance, one of Julius' friends was called "The Professor." Before long, Julius became "The Doctor."

The coach at Roosevelt was a man named Ray Wilson. He saw that Julius had a big future in the game. Just one thing worried him. "Even in the ninth grade Julius was very well coordinated," said Wilson. "The only worry I had about him was his size. He was only 5-10 as a sophomore. But he had those big hands that showed he probably would grow. Luckily I was right about that."

But Coach Wilson was not only impressed by Julius the basketball player. He was impressed by Julius the person as well. "Julius' family always took a healthy interest in him," said the coach, "and he never was affected adversely by his success. In addition, he took out his natural aggressions on the basketball court rather than in a less socially acceptable place."

There was a lot of truth to that. Julius admitted that basketball was sometimes real medicine for him. "If I had an argument or something at home, I didn't get angry and yell and scream. I just got my stuff and went over to the playground to play ball. That worked it all out of my system."

Julius slowly became a star at Roosevelt. By his senior year he was 6-3$\frac{1}{2}$ and still a skinny 165 pounds. But he already had the moves. He averaged nearly 25 points and 17 rebounds a game. He was also a good student. It wasn't surprising that many colleges around the country began offering him scholarships. It would be a tough decision for the youngster to make.

"When I started getting all those offers, I decided to make a little trip," he said. "So I went out west and visited Iowa State and Ohio State. I didn't like either one and decided to stay in the East.

"Of course, there were several good city schools. But I figured there would be too many distractions in the city. I was interested in my education and in becoming a better basketball player."

That's when Julius began looking toward New England. He liked the area up there. He learned about several schools, including Dartmouth, Amherst, Boston University, Rhode Island, Connecticut and the University of Massachusetts. Finally it was between Amherst and the University of Massachusetts. Julius chose U. Mass because the coach there, Jack Leaman, was a close friend of Ray Wilson. It was also a school with a good academic program. Julius knew he'd get a good education.

"I also knew I wouldn't be used at Massachusetts," he said. "I trusted the people there. In addition, the basketball program was rising. I knew I'd have a good chance to start as a sophomore."

The University of Massachusetts played in the Yankee Conference against other schools from the area. Very few future pro players come from there. It's not really big-time basketball. But that didn't bother Julius.

"I just wanted to play somewhere and enjoy it while I got my education," he said. "If a ballplayer is good enough to make it, he'll make

Julius poses on the U. Mass. basketball court with his coach there, Jack Leaman.

it. And it won't matter if he's at U. Mass or UCLA."

But before Julius began his college career, there was a personal tragedy in his life. His younger brother, Marvin, just 16, died suddenly of a rare disease. The death was taken very hard by Julius and the rest of his family.

It was years later when Julius finally talked about it. "My brother's death is still on my mind a lot," he said. "We were always a close family, and my mother had worked very hard to make us all comfortable. But during that period everything changed so quickly. Marvin died. Then my sister got married. Then I went away to college. Suddenly my mother was without her kids for the first time. I always thought about that time, and I guess I always pushed a little harder because of it."

Julius entered U. Mass as a

freshman in September 1968. He was very popular right from the start. He had a very likeable personality and a good word for everyone. He also tried to excel at everything he did, and people respected him for that. Then when they saw him play basketball, he really won them over.

The Doctor was playing freshman ball that first year. Suddenly huge crowds were coming out to see the freshmen play. Some of the people would even leave before the varsity game started. They came, of course, to watch Julius. They were even on hand when the team warmed up.

That was because Julius would go through his vast array of dunk shots during warm-ups. The crowd screamed and yelled as though a championship game were in the works. One time he went high above the basket for a two-hand, over-the-head dunk and received a standing ovation.

Then on February 22, 1969, the night of Julius' 19th birthday, the big crowd stood on its feet and sang Happy Birthday to him. "It was really an exciting thing," he recalls. "Nothing like that had ever happened to me before. I got goose bumps from it."

Julius repaid the faithful fans, however. He led the U. Mass frosh to the first unbeaten season in their history. Now he was ready for the varsity.

CHAPTER THREE

"A PH.D. IN BASKETBALL"

U. Mass didn't have a great team in 1969-70. The players in general weren't that good. But the Doctor was. He was getting closer to his full height of 6-7 and could fly through the air. He could go high above the backboard to rebound, and he seemed to hang in the air longer than anyone when he drove. His outside shot was improving, too. College rules didn't allow the slam-dunk then, so Julius could show his magic dunks only in practice and warm-ups.

But thanks to Julius, the U.Mass Minutemen were winning. They didn't have the personnel to play a wide-open game, but Julius later said he had learned many things from the U.Mass style of play.

When the regular season ended, U.Mass had made a fine 18-6 mark, and Julius had broken many school records. He averaged 25.7 points a game and pulled down an average of 20.9 rebounds. That rebounding average was really something. It placed Julius second in the entire nation. The man who led in rebounding was Artis Gilmore of Jacksonville. And he was seven feet, two inches tall!

Some people still claimed that Julius wasn't that good. They said that U.Mass played against other small schools and that Julius wouldn't do so well if he were at a bigger school. But the men who really knew the game felt otherwise. In 1969-70, Julius was New England's Player of the Year, All-East Sophomore of the Year, and an honorable mention All-America.

Coach Jack Leaman was one of Julius' biggest fans. "I can't believe there's a better sophomore in the whole country," said Leaman. "And people see only half of Julie's ability—his scoring and rebounding. But he can do so many other things. He can make the super pass like a Bob Cousy. And he has those great big hands. He can hit a man at three-quarter court when we fast-break, and he plays excellent defense. And when a player his size is ranked second nationally in rebounding, he has to be doing something right."

Mainly because of Julius, the Minutemen were asked to play in the National Invitational Tournament (NIT) at Madison Square Garden in New York City. The NIT took place at the end of the regular season. It usually has had some of the best teams in the country.

As luck would have it, the Minutemen drew a very tough opponent in their first game. They had to play Marquette University, the top-rated team in the whole tourney. It was a hard-fought game all the way. With Julius playing great at both ends of the court, U.Mass stayed in the game. But at the end Marquette was too strong. The Warriors won, 62-55. From there, they went on to win the tournament. And their game with U.Mass was the closest they played.

The Doctor scored 31 points in this 79-67 win over Colgate in 1970.

At least New York fans finally had a chance to see Julius play. Even though he was from the area, it was the first time he had ever played in Madison Square Garden.

His next basketball adventure was far from the Garden. That summer he was a member of the U.S. National team that went to play in Russia and Eastern Europe.

"That trip was a once-in-a-lifetime thing," Julius said later. "I've had a lot of good times in my life, but that was really something special. I saw how people in other parts of the world lived and learned what they were like. It was just as I thought it would be as a kid. Basketball gave me the chance really to see and do things I couldn't have done otherwise."

Number 32 rises to the occasion once again as he taps in a basket against St. Anselm in 1970. Julius scored 32 points that night and U. Mass. won the game 98-63.

There was one minor problem. Julius hurt his back before the tour ended. But it was all right before his junior year began. There were many predictions about the best college players in the upcoming season. As expected, Julius wasn't listed by too many of the writers. They just hadn't seen him play. But when Jack Leaman saw his star missing from the headlines, he was furious.

"Julie is one of the best players in the nation," Leaman said. "He has to go early in the pro draft. And he'll not only be a good pro, he'll be a great pro. He's worked hard to get where he is today, and he can handle any situation, whether it concerns basketball or his personal life. Plus he's such a great team player that there has never been any resentment from the rest of the team. They proved it by electing him co-captain for this year."

The Doctor still played it cool about his lack of recognition, but he felt the team should get more notice.

"We had a very strong team in 1970-71," he said. "I'm sorry we didn't have an independent schedule that would have let us play some of the more famous teams in the country. But we had to stick to the conference schedule. As for myself, I knew I was as good as some of the guys who got more attention. I just wanted to play as well as I could and help the team win."

The Minutemen did a lot of winning that year. They won 23 of the 26 games they played. It was the best record in the school's history. And they generally won big. Their average margin of victory that year was 14.6 points a game.

Julius was absolutely brilliant all year. He did whatever it took to win—scoring, rebounding, passing, playing defense. Even though he still played at U.Mass, it was hard to imagine a better college forward. That's what Julius' old high school coach, Ray Wilson, thought. He saw the Doctor play a few times and then talked about his former star.

"Each time I see him, he does something I've never seen him do before," said Wilson, "so I can't help thinking he's going to get even better. I watch a player like Sidney Wicks [then at UCLA], who's thought of as the best college forward in the country. He's very quick and goes to the offensive board very well. So does Julius. Then I think maybe Julius can shoot from a deeper position. Suddenly I find myself thinking, 'Is Julius in the same class as a ballplayer like Wicks?' The answer has to be yes!"

Julius' numbers were again impressive. He averaged 26.9 points and 19.5 rebounds a game. The one sour note was the NIT. The Minutemen were invited to the New York tourney once again. This time they were trounced by a powerful North Carolina team, 90-49. It didn't matter that the Tar Heels went on to win the tourney. U.Mass had a bad game at the worse time. But all in all, it had been a great year.

Now it seemed as if Julius could relax and look forward to his senior year. But because some things about professional sports were changing, that wouldn't happen. In the past, the pro basketball leagues didn't draft college players until their class had graduated. But in 1971 things were different. The American Basketball Association was trying to get all the good college players it could. To do this, it was picking college players who still had one or two years of college left.

Julius races the ball up the court at the Rucker Tourney in New York's Harlem in 1972.

This put a great deal of pressure on Julius. Several pro teams began scouting him during his junior year. Before the year was over, they began asking him if he would leave school and sign a pro contract. Julius had come to Massachusetts for an education. He had been a good student. But he also knew he was ready for the pros. If he signed, he could help his family right away. Who knows what another year would bring?

"Yeah, I'm ready to be thrown into deep water," he said, "and I think I'm ready to swim."

The team Julius really wanted to play for was the New York Nets. They had a brand new arena, the Nassau Veterans Memorial Coliseum. It was located just a few miles from where the Doctor had grown up. Wouldn't it be great if Julius could play in his own backyard!

There was just one problem. The Nets coach, Lou Carnesecca, still didn't feel it was right to sign players who still had time in college. He felt that if all the teams started doing this, the entire system would be ruined. So the Nets announced they would not sign college players whose class had not graduated.

That left Julius out in the cold. But not for long. He quickly reached a decision. He announced he was leaving U.Mass to sign with the Virginia Squires of the ABA.

"An agent called me during Easter recess," Julius remembers. "He talked and I listened. Then I signed for four years at $500,000."

It was certainly a lot of money, though not as much as he would be making a few years later. Everyone at the New England school was sorry to see him leave. Especially Coach Leaman. But the coach

After the Rucker Tourney, Julius takes some time out to talk to his young fans about the value of education and self-development.

35

The Doctor is driving for a basket and is not going to be stopped at a summer tournament in 1973.

knew Julius was doing what he had to do.

That summer Julius played in the Holcombe Rucker Memorial Playground Tournament in Harlem. Harlem is one of the black communities in New York City. The Rucker Tourney, as it is called, has some of the great playground players and great pros alike. It's a showcase tourney where the different players love to show their moves. Well, no one has more moves than the Doctor. He took the tourney by storm. He showed moves many tournament veterans had never even dreamed of before.

Julius' coach that summer was Floyd Layne, a former college star and coach at CCNY in New York. Layne quickly became still another die-hard Erving fan. "The thing that makes him so great is his tremendous imagination," said

Layne. "He has more moves than Bobby Fischer [a chess champion]. Julius is Earl Monroe with size and power."

Others said that no one could do more things in mid-air since the heyday of Connie Hawkins. Hawkins was a former playground and pro star. Game after game, the Doctor showed the crowds new things. In one game he scored 54 points. And when it was over, he was named the tourney's Most Valuable Player.

"They were all reflex moves," said Julius, modestly. "But I enjoyed the crowds there. I think it's great when the fans get involved in the game. Still, I don't go out of my way to be a showboat."

CHAPTER FOUR

ABA ROOKIE OF THE YEAR

From there, Julius went to join his new pro team, the Squires. And he was ready. He was coming to a pretty good team. The year before, the Squires had a 55-29 record, best mark in the league. And they already had a superstar in guard Charlie Scott. Scott was a thin, 6-6 backcourt man who loved to run and shoot. It was the same kind of game Julius liked to play. The two

worked well right from the outset. Julius won a starting job in training camp and opened the season at forward. One trip around the league and he had people talking.

"I've been around a long time," said referee Earl Strom. "I've seen them come and go in both leagues. But I've never seen one like him. I just worked an exhibition game, and Erving showed me moves I've never seen experienced men make, much less a rookie."

And Julius' new coach, former NBA star Al Bianchi, had more good words to say. "With a little more experience, Julius will be the best forward who ever played the game. Absolutely the best. The only one who compares with Julius is Elgin Baylor. They both have great body control. Julie can put the

Julius is still wearing Number 32 here, but now it's for the Virginia Squires instead of U. Mass.

ball down as well as Baylor, he can shoot as well, can run better, can rebound better, play defense a heck of a lot better, and Julie can shoot with either hand."

That wasn't all. The other players were beginning to take note. Veteran forward Cincy Powell of Kentucky had the job of guarding Julius one night. Powell was known as a tough defensive player. But after the game he couldn't stop talking about the rookie from U. Mass.

"He's too much for me to handle," said Powell. "He has great one-on-one moves. I had heard he was good, but I didn't think he was that good. He's only 21 years old now and I'd hate to think of what he's gonna be like when he gets a couple more years of experience."

The Squires had some other young players in the lineup during

1971-72. The team was making mistakes. They weren't winning quite as often as the year before. They didn't have a top center and the bench was weak. Charlie Scott was having a great year, though. He was leading the ABA in scoring by hitting nearly 35 points a game. Julius wasn't that far behind. He was around the 25-point mark and was leading the team in rebounding. They were the most powerful one-two punch in the league.

A game against the New York Nets midway through the season showed the two stars at their best. It took Virginia two overtimes to win it, 137-113. Scott had 42 points. Julius wasn't far behind. He scored 29 and grabbed a game high of 17 rebounds. And he played only 37 minutes!

"Julius is just what we thought he'd be," crowed Coach

Bianchi after the game. "If he had played another year of college ball, he would have been one of the two or three top picks in the country. And we never would have had a chance at him."

Julius himself admitted, "I caught everyone by surprise. That helped me a great deal. In other words, no one was sick and tired reading about my college career. And more importantly, no one knew my moves. So I kind of came into the league cold, an unknown quantity."

But the praise continued from all corners. The Doctor didn't let himself get a big head. Coach Alex Hannum of Denver said, "Julius turns the whole league on. He's the best thing that's happened to it yet. People can't wait for him to come to town again." And Julius kept working hard. He just wanted the Squires to win. But with just a few weeks left in the season, the team got a big shock.

They learned that Charlie Scott was leaving. He was jumping to an NBA team, the Phoenix Suns. So with 11 games left in the season, the Squires had lost the league's top scorer. That put even more pressure on the Doctor. He suddenly found himself the team leader. Before Scott left, Julius worked mostly on the inside. Now Coach Bianchi told him to shoot from anyplace on the floor.

Julius did very well those last weeks. But the Squires final record was only 45-39. They were far behind Kentucky, which had a mighty 68-16 mark. Still, they were in the playoffs.

The Doctor finished his rookie year as the sixth best scorer in the league with 2,290 points and a 27.3 average. He also grabbed 1,319 rebounds for a 15.7 average. That was third best in the league. There was little surprise when he was named ABA Rookie of the Year.

In the playoffs, Julius was even better. Virginia beat Miami four straight in the first round. In game three, Julius scored a record 53 points. In the other series, the New York Nets surprised everyone by whipping league champ Kentucky. Now Virginia had to play New York, with the winner going to the finals.

Once again the young Nets surprised everyone. The series took seven games, but the New Yorkers won the last one, 94-88, despite some great play by the Doctor. In 11 playoff games, Julius averaged 33.3 points and an amazing 20.4 rebounds. He had surely emerged as one of the great stars of the league.

When the season ended, Julius talked about pro ball. He explained how it was different from college and the things he had to do to adjust his game.

"First of all, I wasn't a good shooter when I went to college. I practiced shooting before and after my college games, and I did the same thing my rookie year. Even though I was playing inside, I practiced my outside shooting faithfully. It paid off because when Charlie Scott left the team, I found myself shooting from the outside more often.

"Plus in college I just out-jumped everyone. You might say I did my thing in the kitchen and got out. When I started with Virginia, I found the pros doing a lot more shoving and bumping . . . and getting away with it! They never got away with that stuff in college.

"I also found there was a lot more holding in the pro game. I was playing college defense and getting beat. And when I had the ball on offense, I found myself getting held, grabbed, kicked . . . you name it."

But the Doctor soon found a remedy for these things. "Some of them [the holders] I just outran, using my speed to the fullest advantage. Other times I just rolled with the punches. It took me awhile really to learn pro defense and how to protect myself on offense. You have to learn these things or you'll wind up with an injury."

So it looked as though Julius was ready for a long career in Virginia. But before the next season began, there was trouble. Julius felt the Squires weren't living up to their promises. Much of the money he signed for was to be paid him later. He felt he should be getting more of it up front. He said he hadn't received any bonus and not that much of his salary.

The truth was the Virginia team was losing money, as were many ABA teams. The owners might not have been able to pay Julius more even if they wanted to. The whole thing made the Doctor uneasy. He began to look elsewhere. He even went as far as to sign a contract with the Atlanta Hawks of the NBA. But Virginia took the case to court. After playing a few exhibition games with the Hawks, the Doctor was ordered to return to the Squires.

When the courts ruled that Julius had to play for Virginia he didn't argue. "I have to play there now, so that's what I'm going to do. I'll worry about the future later."

The Squires team really had its problems in 1972-73. Scott was gone, of course, and there were many young players in camp. As Julius said, "I was practically an old-timer on that team."

Though the Doctor quickly jumped into the league scoring lead, the team stayed at around the .500 mark. While Kentucky and Carolina battled it out for first place in the division, Virginia could do no better than third with a 42-42 record. Julius led the league in scoring with a 31.9 mark. He was also sixth in rebounding. But team spirit wasn't good. Despite a great personal year, the Doctor wanted to get out of Virginia.

In the playoffs, the Squires were beaten easily by Kentucky in five games. Now Julius had time to think about his future. He had seen what the addition of former NBA star Billy Cunningham had done for Carolina. He liked that.

"Billy did a little bit of everything for the Cougars," said Julius. "He scored, rebounded, blocked shots, stole the ball, ran the fast break, played defense. He took that team from fifth to first in one season. He played team ball and made them into a team. That's what I'd like to do in this sport, become part of a real team situation."

There was something that Julius didn't know then. The Virginia team was still losing money. They knew Julius would leave as soon as he legally could. So they were looking to make a deal for him that would bring the team some money.

Dr. J seems happy to be returning to New York as Nets' president Ray Boe makes the announcement in 1973.

CHAPTER FIVE

THE NETS "A GREAT EXPERIENCE"

On August 1, 1973, a deal was announced. Julius was being sold to the New York Nets. It was the team he had always wanted to play for. And ABA officials thought that the move was good for the league. The money part of the deal was very complex. Julius' new contract was for seven years and worth about $1.9 million.

So a very happy Julius reported to the Nets for the 1973-74 season. It was a young team, with a new young coach in Kevin Loughery. There was an exciting rookie in 6-9 forward Larry Kenon, a good center in 6-11 Billy Paultz. There was also a good backcourt with speedy Brian Taylor, veterans John Roche and Billy Melchionni, and a tough 6-2 rookie named John Williamson. The Nets with the Doctor had a chance to go right to the top.

At the beginning of the season, the 11-man Nets team had an average age of just 22.6 years. They were one of the youngest teams in all of pro sports. But Julius couldn't have been happier with the way things worked out. "I feel this is going to be a great experience for me and this team," he said. "I can do the things that will help us win, and the other guys feel it, too. That's just as important."

SLAM-DUNK—Dr. J has done it again, this time against his old team, the Virginia Squires.

The Doctor's first game as a Net was disappointing. The team lost to Indiana, 118-99. But no one could blame Julius. He tossed in a game high of 42 points. His Nets career was underway.

Two nights later, the team got its first win, beating Virginia, 116-105. Next the Nets whipped Carolina, then Memphis, then Utah, Julius getting 33 in that one. The club was 4-1 and in first place. It seemed almost too good to be true.

It was. First the club lost to Kentucky, then dropped a pair to San Antonio. Then they were beaten by Denver. Then Kentucky topped then again. Another loss to Kentucky made it six in a row.

Nothing helped. Losses to Virginia, Utah, and San Diego followed. That was nine in a row. The team was 4-10. They seemed to be coming apart. As guard Brian Taylor said, "There was no communication. We were all so distant. And Kevin just yelled a lot, and all that yelling wasn't helping to change things."

Coach Loughery himself recalls that time: "I was an emotional player and I thought it would be good to get my team emotional, too. It got to the point that I was putting the screaming on for the team's benefit. I thought it would work because we were so young. But yelling and screaming doesn't work. The players already had confidence. It took me a while, but I finally realized the problem. It was our defense. We were playing the wrong kind of defense."

So Coach Loughery abandoned the pressing defense he had been using. Instead, the team used a straight man-to-man. The coach also put rookie Williamson into the starting lineup. His toughness on defense helped. And that made vet Billy Melchionni a good sixth man.

During the losing streak, the Doctor was playing his usual game. He was outstanding. He was scoring well and making his dazzling moves. Crowds came to watch him in every city. They cheered loudly when he made one of his great slam-dunks. But as Coach Loughery said, having Julius on the team might have been part of the problem early in the year.

"You get a guy like Doc," said the coach, "and suddenly you're supposed to win. Maybe some of the guys felt that all we needed to do was watch Doc operate. Maybe I was getting to be that way too before we made the changes."

Finally on November 11, the Nets broke the streak. They beat San

Antonio, 106-94. As usual, the Doctor led the way. This time he had 29 points and 12 rebounds.

A few weeks later in a game against the Colonels, the Nets trailed 68-60 with just nine minutes left. Coach Loughery called a time out.

"The way this game was going," he said, "I told Doc he was going to have to pull it out for us."

The orders were to play a tight defense and then give the ball to Julius. And the Doctor began operating. He hit on a twisting drive. Then on a long jumper. Then he soared through the air for a slam-dunk. All in all, Julius scored 16 of the team's final 23 points as the Nets came on to win, 83-82. He also made a big effort on defense. In the last second he blocked a Kentucky shot and then got a key rebound so his team could run out the clock.

That game showed the Nets they could play with the best. They felt they were good enough to win the league title. But there was still a long way to go.

Yet they kept winning. Just before the All-Star game that year, the Nets pulled into first place. They had a 34-20 record. And Julius had a big, 46-point game against Carolina. That gave him the league scoring lead over Kentucky's Dan Issel. Julius was averaging nearly 27.5 points a game. He was also eighth in rebounding, eighth in assists, third in blocked shots, and second in steals. There was little doubt about how good he had become.

The Nets were also getting better. The team made a mid-season trade with Kentucky bringing guard Mike Gale and forward Wendell Ladner to the team. In return, the

Denver defenders try to stop the inevitable, but it looks as though the Doctor will score again.

Julius is an avid fan as well as a devoted player. With his wife, Turquoise, here, he takes a chance to watch other athletes do the work.

Nets sent guard John Roche to the Colonels. Both Gale and Ladner gave the team good all-around play off the bench. Both were rugged players and very good on defense. This was just what the Nets needed to become a top, all-around team.

It was also becoming an all-around year for Julius. In a game against Indiana, he scored 40 points and had 11 assists and 10 rebounds. He had hit on 17 of his 22 shots from the floor—great shooting.

Soon after that, the Doctor surprised everyone. He got married. His wife's name was Turquoise Brown. She and Julius kept their wedding a secret. Both of them are really private people who like to spend a lot of time at home. Soon the secret was out and everyone congratulated the newlyweds.

On the court, Julius couldn't hide. Night after night he continued playing the best forward ever seen by many fans. Coach Loughery was amazed how Julius could do so much without hogging the ball and messing up the rest of the team.

Julius and the Nets kept it up right to the end. They finished in first place with a 55-29 mark, two games ahead of Kentucky. After their poor 4-10 start, the team had a 51-19 record the rest of the way. Now it was time for the playoffs.

As for Julius, he won his second scoring title with 2,299 points and a 27.4 average. He also won the ABA's Most Valuable Player award by a large margin. That didn't surprise anyone. Julius had done what he wanted. He had pulled the Nets together into a championship team.

The first round of the playoffs was easy. The Nets breezed past Vir-

The power of Dr. J's slam-dunk looks as though it will tear the net away from the hoop.

ginia, Julius' old team, in five games. Kentucky also swept past Carolina. Now the Nets and the Colonels would meet for the Eastern title. Many people thought they were the two best teams in the league. The winner of this series should become ABA champ.

But what was expected to be a hard-fought series that would go the full seven games never happened. It turned out to be a laugher. The Nets surprised the basketball world by blowing the Colonels off the court. They won four straight—two in New York and two in Kentucky. The scores were 119-106, 99-80, 89-87, and 103-90.

As expected, Julius was the team leader. In the nine playoff games, he had scored 249 points, an average of 27.6. Now he looked for-

Once again Julius finds himself head and shoulders above his competitors.

ward to the series with the Utah Stars. The winner would be ABA champ.

Julius was really turned on for the opening game. He dazzled everyone—the Stars, the fans, even his teammates. He drove, shot, dunked, popped, twisted, re-bounded, passed, stole the ball. He was all over the court in an amazing show. When the smoke cleared, the mighty Doctor had 47 points and the Nets had an 89-85 victory.

In the second game, Julius had 32. This time he got more help and the Nets won easily, 118-94. They seemed to be on the way. The third game was a cliff-hanger. Utah led, 94-91, with just 10 seconds left. The Nets needed a big play. In the ABA it was possible to get three points for a field goal from more

Soaring all alone through the air, the Doctor sinks another one.

than 25 feet out. First Wendell Ladner shot. He missed. But Mike Gale tapped the rebound back to Brian Taylor. Taylor backed behind the three-point line, shot . . . and hit! The Nets had tied the score.

In overtime, Larry Kenon got a hot hand with several quick hoops and the Nets went on to win, 103-100. They were one game away from the title.

Utah won the fourth game, 97-89, as Julius had just 18. Then in the fifth game everyone on the Nets got hot. Kenon had another fine game, as did rookie Williamson. Julius could take it easy as his team slowly pulled away. The Doctor scored only 20 points, but the Nets won, 111-100. They were ABA champions at last!

To cap a great personal season, the Doctor was voted the MVP of the playoffs. He kept quiet in the locker room after the game, but teammate Brian Taylor didn't. He said what most of the Nets were thinking.

"This team has the ability to win a lot more," said Taylor. "We're young and hungry, and you'll hear from us again." Then he pointed over at the Doctor. "And there's the guy who'll do it for us, too."

When the next season started, it looked as though the Nets would blow everyone out. They were winning and winning big, in first place most of the year. But the last month of the season they faltered. Their record was still better than the year before, 58-26. But they were tied by Kentucky and lost a one-game playoff for the Eastern title.

For Julius it was another fine year. He averaged 27.8 points, but he didn't win the scoring title. Still,

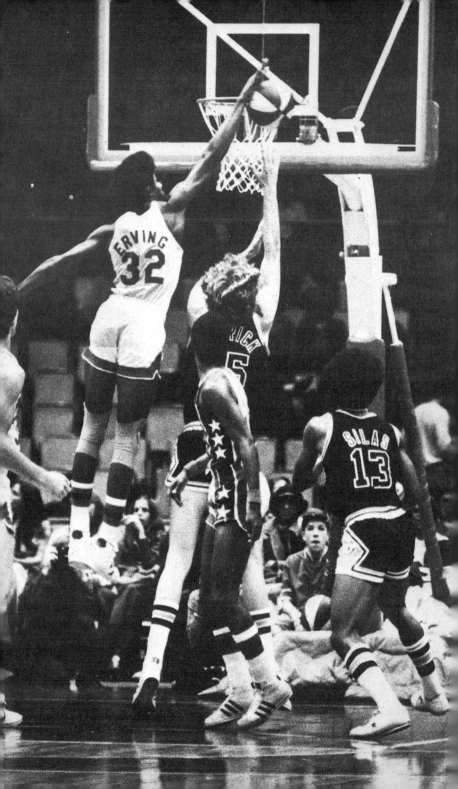

he looked forward to the playoffs. In the first round, the Nets would meet the Spirits of St. Louis, a team they had beaten 12 straight during the regular season.

But something happened. The Spirits suddenly caught fire and the Nets were flat. They stayed flat. The Spirits won the series in five games. The Nets were out of it. It was one of the big upsets in sports history.

Dr. J, as usual, is the first one up for the rebound.

CHAPTER SIX

THE MOST EXCITING PLAYER IN THE GAME

It was hard to say what was wrong. The team played well most of the year. But Net officials wanted changes. Perhaps it was a mistake, but the club traded Paultz, Kenon and Mike Gale to San Antonio for forward Rich Jones, centers Swen Nater and Kim Hughes and another forward, Chuck Terry.

The ABA was also in trouble during the 1975-76 season. Several teams folded as the season progressed. Soon there were just six teams left. They were put in one big division and played each other many times. It was obvious that the league was in deep trouble.

Despite the trade, the Nets were playing well. Julius, in fact, was having perhaps his most brilliant season. He was doing it all better than ever before. He dazzled whatever ABA fans were left. He was, perhaps, the only man in the league who could draw a crowd.

The Doctor regained the scoring title with 2,462 points and a 29.3 average. He became the league's MVP for the third straight year. The Nets finished with a 55-29 mark, second to Denver in the one-division league. In the first round of the playoffs, they had to face San Antonio.

The Nets won the first game,

*After the Nets won the ABA championship in 1976,
Julius got a real champagne treatment—in the hair
as well as in the mouth.*

then dropped the next two to the Spurs. But they bounced back with a pair of 110-108 wins to take a 3-2 lead. San Antonio tied it with a 106-105 victory. Each game was close and exciting. Then in the seventh game the Nets won it, 121-114, with Julius playing brilliantly.

Now it was Denver, the league's best team. That's when the Doctor went to work. He had 45 points in the opener as the Nets won, 120-118. In game two he was even better, with 49 points. But Denver came on to win it, 127-121. Yet Julius' play inspired his teammates. They rallied behind him to win the next two, 117-11 and 121-112.

Denver came on to win game five, 118-110, but in game six Julius and the Nets did it, winning 112-106, to take the ABA title once again. Julius averaged 34.6 points in

13 playoff games and also nabbed 164 rebounds. It was as though he were showing everyone once again that he was the best in the business. He didn't know it then, but it was to be the last time he'd put on a Nets uniform.

During the offseason two things happened. The ABA finally folded and the NBA took in four of the teams—Denver, San Antonio, Indiana and the Nets. The other players were drafted by NBA teams. The second thing was a big Nets trade. The team sent Brian Taylor to Kansas City for All-Star guard Nate "Tiny" Archibald, one of the NBA greats. Now fans couldn't wait to see Tiny and the Doctor on the same team.

But perhaps that's what started the trouble. Archibald was one of the most highly paid players in the game. He was earning quite a bit more than Julius. Soon after the trade, the Doctor told the Nets he wanted his contract rewritten. And when the Nets refused, the holdout began.

Many people were angry at Julius. They felt he was not being loyal, that he was selling out. He was already earning a great deal of money. But then his agent pointed out that there were at least 25 NBA players earning more. And Julius claimed the Nets had broken some promises.

It's hard to say who is right and who is wrong. One thing is certain. The Doctor was the most exciting player in the game. And he knew that NBA people were using him. They were building their TV schedule around him and the Nets. Almost all teams were advertising the Nets games and the Doctor. They knew that NBA fans were very

anxious to see him play. So in a sense, many people around the league were planning to make money off Julius' talents. Maybe he should have been paid more.

At the same time, the Nets needed money. They had to pay a lot to join the NBA, and they also had to pay a lot to the Knicks, the NBA team in New York. Those were league rules. Then when they got Archibald, they had to pay him. So some felt they just didn't have the money to give the Doctor a new contract.

And so it went until the surprise announcement came. Julius was traded to the 76ers. It was hard to believe. He was going to a team that already had a superstar forward, George McGinnis. So the

The Bicentennial Year's $6-million-dollar man— $3.5 million for Julius and $3 million for the Nets for selling him to the Philadelphia 76ers.

Doctor would have to share the spotlight.

As the 1976-77 season started, it was obvious things weren't the same. The Nets did collapse. With the Doctor gone, there was no scoring up front. Archibald and John Williamson had to carry the load. Then in early January, Tiny broke his foot. The Nets were destined to fall to last place.

At the same time, Julius was having a hard time blending with his mates. The 76ers were in first place, but not by much. Like some other teams with many good players, they really weren't working together. Julius even complained near midseason that the club didn't have a leader and that some of the players wouldn't listen to him.

Moneywise, the Doctor got his wish. His new contract with the

Two of basketball's superstars, George McGinnis and Julius Erving—both on the 76ers squad.

(Above) As Dr. J goes up and under, the Bullets can do nothing but watch.
(Opposite) The Chicago Bulls seem to be asking, "What's going to happen now? as Julius bats the ball away.

84

(Above) Dr. J is clear all the way as he goes slam-dunk against Indiana.
(Opposite) The tireless rebounder is after the ball again.

76ers was said to be worth $3.5 million for six years. He had become the most highly paid player in the game. But he had also paid a price. Some of his great artistry was gone. After the Nets had won their first ABA title in 1973-74, Coach Kevin Loughery had said, "Julius is the greatest player I've ever been around. But he's more than that, a lot more. He's one of the greatest people I've ever been around. He's really a super person."

The same Loughery saw the Doctor play with the 76ers several times early in the 1976 season. He refused to say anything bad about Julius for leaving the Nets. But he did see changes.

"Doc did a lot for me and a lot of other people here," said Loughery. "I still say he's one of the

Julius Erving has thousands of fans, but perhaps none better than these two small Ervings.

greatest people I've known. It really hurts me to see him now. He's not enjoying the game anymore. He doesn't have that bright look in his eye. And he's surely not doing the things he can do.

"The fans are losing out as well because they can no longer see the greatest show in basketball. It just isn't there. It can't be there in his present situation."

The Doctor still has the talents. He's only 27, in his absolute prime. If he can't get it together with the 76ers, all the money in the world might not matter. For the Doctor is an artist, and an artist must do his thing. The Nets were his team. He could do it all. Now he's just a forward with the 76ers. Whether or not he's given a chance to become the Doctor of old, only time will tell. Basketball fans everywhere hope that he does.